Contents

More important than the quest for certainty
is the quest for clarity.

— Francois Gautier

1. Exploring the Quantum Mysteries

Within the realm of quantum physics, a fascinating yet perplexing element emerges: the Quantum Zero-Point Field. While it may sound like an esoteric concept reserved for physicists and theoreticians, its implications touch every fiber of the universe around us, harboring secrets that could revolutionize technology, energy, and even the foundational understanding of reality itself. This book, "The Emptiness Full of Everything," aims to make the intricacies of the Zero-Point Field accessible to curious minds, bridging the gap between advanced science and everyday understanding. Join me on this voyage as we unravel the layers of scientific discoveries, historical insights, and potential future technologies, all encapsulated within this astonishing field of energy and mystery. Whether you're a student of science, an enthusiastic layman, or simply driven by curiosity, this journey promises to open doors to possibilities you had never considered, hinting at realms where emptiness is a gateway to infinite energy, and silence echoes with the pulse of the cosmos.

2. Understanding the Origins

2.1. Emergence of Quantum Physics

The origins of quantum physics can be traced back to the early 20th century, a time characterized by profound transformations in scientific thought. The unraveling of nature's mysteries urged physicists from the confines of classical concepts toward a domain that defied traditional logic and intuition. Classical physics, which had dominated for centuries, was built upon deterministic frameworks; it offered equations that could predict the movements of planets, the trajectories of projectiles, and the behavior of gases. However, this era faced significant challenges as the behavior of matter at tiny scales showed discrepancies that classical laws could not account for.

The quest for understanding began with the foundational work of Max Planck, who in 1900 proposed the idea of quantization. While studying blackbody radiation, he discovered that energy could not be absorbed or emitted continuously, but rather in discrete packets, which he termed 'quanta.' This revolutionary idea suggested that light, once thought to behave solely as a wave, also possessed particle-like properties. The implications of this duality laid the groundwork for quantum theory. As physicists absorbed Planck's revolutionary insights, it became increasingly evident that a new set of rules governed the microcosm, challenging the very fabric of classical mechanics.

As Planck's ideas gained traction, another monumental figure, Albert Einstein, further contributed to the quantum landscape. In 1905, he famously explained the photoelectric effect by positing that light itself is composed of quanta, later called photons. This work not only validated the particle theory of light but also established a precedent for the duality of nature; light could no longer be categorized strictly as a wave or a particle but rather as both depending on the context of observation. Einstein's contributions were pivotal, both in cementing the necessity for quantum mechanics and in provoking philosophical discussions about the nature of reality itself.

The emergence of quantum physics did not occur in isolation but was characterized by vibrant debates between leading scientists. Niels Bohr, Werner Heisenberg, and Erwin Schrödinger, among others, participated in spirited discussions that ignited the foundations of what would become quantum mechanics. Bohr introduced the model of the atom that incorporated quantum principles, with electrons existing in probabilistic orbits rather than fixed paths. This concept fully strayed from the deterministic reality of classical physics, suggesting a universe shrouded in uncertainty and probability. Meanwhile, Heisenberg articulated his uncertainty principle, asserting limits to the precision with which pairs of physical properties could be known simultaneously. These radical ideas caused a seismic shift in the scientific landscape, forcing physicists to re-evaluate their understanding of measurements, observations, and the nature of information itself.

Another critical aspect of quantum emergence was the transition away from deterministic views. The classical universe was one where future states were entirely predictable given a set of initial conditions. However, the new quantum mechanics signaled a universe where inherent uncertainty reigned supreme. This transition found its expression in mathematical formulations and experiments that demonstrated phenomena impossible to explain within classical frameworks, such as quantum entanglement, wave-particle duality, and superposition.

The groundwork laid by these early explorations culminated in what is popularly known as the quantum revolution. This period witnessed a profound rethinking of fundamental physics and the philosophical implications thereof. Scientists could no longer rely on the visualizations and intuitive ideas of classical physics; instead, they had to embrace a new logic that acknowledged that particles could exist in multiple states simultaneously and that observation itself could influence reality.

Through this remarkable journey, quantum physics emerged not only as a new branch of science but as a transformative force altering humanity's understanding of the universe. The conceptual landscape expanded, giving rise to more complex theories and applications while simultaneously inviting philosophical inquiries about determinism, reality, and human cognition. The fabric of existence began to appear more intricate, interwoven with the delicate threads of probability, revealing a cosmos pulsing with potentialities rather than certainties.

As the 20th century progressed, the broader implications of quantum physics became central to numerous advancements; the genesis of quantum field theory and developments in atomic and subatomic physics established a platform for modern technologies. The emergence of quantum physics, rooted in the defiance of classical reasoning, thus set the stage for a future where the mysteries of the Quantum Zero-Point Field would eventually instigate further explorations into the nature of energy, matter, and the cosmos itself.

In reflecting on the emergence of quantum physics, one recognizes that it represents more than just a historical shift in scientific understanding. It embodies the human spirit's relentless quest to grasp the fundamental principles governing the universe. As this field continues to evolve, the echoes of its origins remind us of the intricate dance between mystery and knowledge, urging us to explore even further into the depths of the Quantum Zero-Point Field and its far-reaching implications. This exploration not only enriches our grasp of the physical world but also hints at deeper truths about the relationship between consciousness, existence, and the vast potential of the universe we inhabit.

2.2. Notable Figures in Quantum Theory

Max Planck, often regarded as the father of quantum theory, set the stage for a monumental shift in how scientists understand the universe. Born in Germany in 1858, Planck's work in thermodynamics and blackbody radiation led him to propose that energy is quantized. He introduced the concept of energy quanta, suggesting that energy could only be released or absorbed in discrete units rather than in a continuous flow. This groundbreaking idea emerged from his studies of blackbody radiation, which could not be satisfactorily explained by the classical physics of his time. He expressed this quantization mathematically through his now-famous equation, $E=hf$, where E is energy, h is Planck's constant, and f is frequency. This radical departure from classical physics not only garnered attention but also laid the groundwork for future developments in quantum mechanics.

Planck's theories were met with initial resistance from his contemporaries, primarily because they challenged the very principles underlying classical physics. However, as more empirical evidence accumulated, particularly through experiments related to the photoelectric effect and atomic spectroscopy, his ideas gained credibility. The implications of Planck's work were nothing short of revolutionary, leading to the birth of quantum mechanics, which fundamentally transformed our comprehension of physical reality.

Following Planck, Albert Einstein emerged as one of the most influential figures in the realm of quantum theory. His contributions, particularly in explaining the photoelectric effect in 1905, suggested that light behaves not only as a wave but also as a stream of particles called photons. This dual nature of light enthralled the scientific community and cemented the concept that elementary particles exhibit both wave-like and particle-like characteristics, further challenging classical notions of physics. Einstein's assertion that the energy carried by these photons is proportional to their frequency—expressed in the now widely acknowledged equation $E=hf$—emphasized the quantum nature of light and helped validate Planck's earlier models.

What distinguishes Einstein's contributions from Planck's was his philosophical approach to quantum theory. He instigated debates on the implications of quantum mechanics, particularly on determinism and the nature of reality. Einstein famously stated that "God does not play dice with the universe," reflecting his discomfort with the inherent randomness found in quantum mechanics. This philosophical stance led to a critical discourse, with Einstein advocating for a deterministic worldview while others, like Niels Bohr, embraced the probabilistic interpretations stemming from quantum theory.

Niels Bohr, a Danish physicist and another luminary in quantum theory, played a pivotal role in the development of the Copenhagen interpretation of quantum mechanics. Bohr's model of the atom, developed in 1913, introduced the idea of quantized energy levels, which posited that electrons exist in specific energy states. His concept of complementarity illustrated that objects in the quantum realm can exhibit both particle and wave characteristics, depending on how they are observed. This drove home the interplay between measurement, observation, and the behavior of particles, suggesting that the act of observation is fundamentally tied to the nature of reality. Bohr's debates with Einstein, particularly during the Solvay Conferences, helped refine the philosophical and conceptual underpinnings of quantum theory.

Another significant figure in this landscape was Werner Heisenberg, known for his formulation of the uncertainty principle in 1927. Heisenberg's principle articulated a fundamental limit to the precision with which certain pairs of physical properties (like position and momentum) can be known simultaneously. This idea signaled a departure from classical determinism, reinforcing the notion that the universe operates on probabilistic outcomes rather than predictable certainties. Heisenberg's concepts laid a foundation for matrix mechanics and contributed to the broader understanding of quantum behaviors.

Erwin Schrödinger, a contemporary of Bohr and Heisenberg, introduced wave mechanics, presenting a different graphical interpretation of quantum phenomena. His famous Schrödinger equation, formulated in 1926, articulated how the quantum state of a system evolves over time. This equation established a connection between quantum physics and the wave-like behavior of particles, emphasizing the centrality of the wave function in describing the probabilistic nature of particles and their interactions. Schrödinger's work opened new avenues for understanding the dynamics of quantum systems and further complicated the philosophical interpretations of consciousness and reality.

These notable figures created a rich tapestry of ideas and debates, each contributing to the synthesis of thought that would characterize quantum mechanics. The rise of these scientists not only elucidated the principles underlying quantum phenomena but also captivated the imagination of their contemporaries and future generations alike. Their collaborative and often contentious dialogues became fundamental in shaping what we understand as quantum theory today.

The implications of their collective work extended beyond the confines of theoretical physics; they fostered explorations in the realms of philosophy, technology, and even the arts. These debates prompted a reevaluation of reality's nature, encouraging subsequent generations of physicists to contemplate the consequences of quantum mechanics in relation to ethics, consciousness, and the underlying fabric of existence. The rich interplay between these scientific minds served to illuminate the complexities of a universe governed by quantum probabilities.

As scholars continue to unravel the intricacies of quantum theory, the legacies of figures such as Planck, Einstein, Bohr, Heisenberg, and Schrödinger serve as pillars of inspiration, reminding us of the profound journey into the depths of the Quantum Zero-Point Field. Their work compels us to explore potentialities woven into the fabric of existence, pondering the role of emptiness in a universe filled with energy, information, and extraordinary possibilities waiting to be unveiled.

2.3. Debates and Developments

The evolution of modern quantum mechanics is deeply rooted in a history characterized by intense debates, groundbreaking discoveries, and shifting paradigms. The trajectory from classical to quantum theories reflects a monumental change in our understanding of the universe, one that transcended the boundaries of traditional physics and ushered in a new era of scientific thought. Examining the historical context surrounding these debates and developments sheds light on how the Quantum Zero-Point Field emerged as a significant concept within this transformative landscape.

At the turn of the 20th century, the scientific community grappled with numerous perplexing phenomena that were beyond the explanatory power of classical physics. As physicists began to observe the discrepancies between experimental results and theoretical predictions, a growing consensus emerged: the existing frameworks were insufficient to account for the complexities of the atomic and subatomic realms. The debates ignited among leading scholars, such as Max Planck, Albert Einstein, Niels Bohr, and later, Werner Heisenberg and Erwin Schrödinger, set the stage for a profound rethinking of fundamental physics.

The uncertainties and contradictions inherent in classical theories sparked spirited discussions known as the quantum debates. Planck's introduction of quantization and Einstein's work on the photoelectric effect challenged long-standing assumptions about light and energy conservation. Einstein's assertion that energy could not be continuous but rather quantized challenged the prevailing Newtonian paradigm, creating tension between those who favored deterministic models and those who embraced the probabilistic nature of quantum mechanics.

One of the most notable controversies lay in the interpretation of the mathematical framework that emerged from these discussions. The Copenhagen interpretation, championed by Niels Bohr and his colleagues, posited that particles do not possess definite properties until they are observed, introducing a fundamental element of randomness into the understanding of physical systems. Conversely, Einstein's insistence on a deterministic universe clashed with this view. The famous Bohr-Einstein debates during the Solvay Conferences became the epitome of this intellectual struggle, highlighting the philosophical implications of quantum theory and its repercussions on concepts of reality and causality.

In 1927, Werner Heisenberg's uncertainty principle introduced a mathematical expression of this newfound complexity, asserting that certain pairs of physical properties cannot simultaneously be known with arbitrary precision. This principle solidified the notion of inherent unpredictability that lay at the heart of quantum mechanics, a stark contrast to the predictable world of classical mechanics. Ultimately, Heisenberg's principle and the probabilistic approaches advocated by Bohr reshaped the discourse around measurement, observation, and the nature of information. Through these debates, the scientific community grappled with fundamental questions about the universe's structure, sparking a critical re-examination of how physicists understood the nature of reality.

As the intrigue around quantum mechanics grew, the development of quantum field theory became a cornerstone for reconciling earlier debates and forming a cohesive framework. Theoretical advancements in the field led to the realization that particles are excitations in their respective fields, and the idea of the Quantum Zero-Point Field emerged as a central theme. This field was seen as a cavernous reservoir of energy that existed even in empty space, representing the basis for fluctuations and virtual particles that manifested at the quantum level.

The inception of quantum field theories, built from the insights gained during these historical debates, paved the way for revolutionary applications and technologies. As the scientific community came to grips with the implications of zero-point energy, applications ranging from energy harvesting to advancements in quantum computing began to take shape, prompting innovative directions in both physics and engineering. Researchers aimed to harness the staggering potential tied to the Zero-Point Field, exploring methodologies for extracting energy and formulating new technologies that could challenge conventional limits.

Amidst this technological ambition, the debates continue. Skepticism remains part and parcel of the scientific inquiry surrounding the Zero-Point Field, as some scholars contest the feasibility of creating systems that can practically exploit this seemingly limitless reservoir of energy. Furthermore, ethical considerations emerged surrounding the implications of new technologies derived from quantum mechanics, focusing on the repercussions of such advancements and raising questions about the sustainability and moral obligations of scientists and technologists as they manipulate these fundamental forces of nature.

Through these dynamic debates and the continuing dialogue surrounding quantum mechanics, we glean a deeper understanding of how the scientific community operates: it is a living organism, comprised of differing philosophies, assertive opinions, and constant re-evaluations of established ideas. Each contribution, each challenge, and each revelation pushes the boundaries of what we know, inviting ongoing inquiry into the nature of reality itself.

The synthesis of ideas that arises from this milieu captures the essence of scientific progress; it thrives on dialogue and contestation, wherein the interplay of differing perspectives ultimately leads to a richer understanding of the universe. The exploration of the Quantum Zero-Point Field encapsulates this journey—a field that beckons understanding, invites skepticism, and offers possibilities that may well redefine our interaction with the cosmos. In tracing the historical trajectories and ongoing debates, one cannot help but appreciate the complexity and depth of matter as it intersects with the vastness of potential energy lingering in the empty spaces around us. Enhanced comprehension of these dynamics solidifies the Quantum Zero-Point Field not just as an abstract theoretical construct, but as a fundamental aspect of our physical reality awaiting deeper engagement and exploration.

2.4. Transition from Classical to Quantum

The transition from classical physics to quantum theory represents one of the most significant paradigm shifts in the history of science. As researchers began to peel back the layers of the universe's complexities, they uncovered a reality far removed from the deterministic, predictable world described by classical physics. The journey from classical to quantum can be viewed through several lenses: the limitations of classical mechanics, the emergence of quantum concepts, and the potent implications these had for scientific perspectives.

Classical physics, rooted in Newtonian mechanics, provided a framework that successfully described the behavior of macroscopic objects and phenomena. It adhered to deterministic principles, where the future state of a system could be precisely predicted if all initial conditions were known. This paradigm thrived during the Enlightenment, bolstered by successes ranging from celestial mechanics to the laws of thermodynamics. However, as physicists began to explore the atomic and subatomic realms, fundamental discrepancies emerged. Experiments involving blackbody radiation, the photoelectric effect, and the behavior of gases indicated that classical mechanics could no longer account for newly observed phenomena.

An exemplary case illustrating the limitations of classical physics was the Ultraviolet Catastrophe. According to classical theories, energy radiated by blackbodies at ultraviolet wavelengths would diverge to infinity, a notion that contradicted empirical observations. The solution, proposed by Max Planck, marked a pivotal moment that initiated the exploration of quantum behavior. Planck's introduction of quantization suggested that energy was emitted or absorbed in discrete packets, challenging the classical continuum and offering a glimpse into a realm governed by probabilities rather than certainties.

As the early impacts of quantum concepts began to take shape, the classical world's monochromatic view of light was shattered. Einstein's work in 1905 on the photoelectric effect embraced Planck's quantum hypothesis, demonstrating that light possessed both wave-like and particle-like properties. This duality encapsulated a fundamental shift in understanding, where the nature of light was not merely a reflection of classical principles but rather an intricate tapestry woven with elements of uncertainty and complexity.

The transition wasn't merely an extension of classical thought, but rather a complete restructuring of the epistemological framework. Niels Bohr's atomic model introduced quantized energy levels, establishing that electrons inhabit specific states rather than traversing classical orbits. This deviation further emphasized the undercurrents of chance that characterized quantum phenomena. Heisenberg's uncertainty principle consolidated the notion that an intrinsic limit exists in our ability to precisely know simultaneous values of paired physical properties. The debate burgeoned between scientists who championed deterministic world views and those who embraced this nascent quantum perspective, leading to vibrant discussions that reshaped the scientific landscape.

The consequences of this transition ran deep, instigating a radical shift in how reality itself was perceived. Where classical physics proposed a universe governed by order, predictability, and absolute truths, quantum theory ushered in an arena marked by potentiality, randomness, and probabilistic outcomes. The very act of observing a quantum system could influence its behavior, revealing a complex interdependence between observer and observed, fostering questions about the nature of reality and consciousness itself.

As quantum theory gained momentum, physicists began conceiving of the universe not as a mechanical clockwork but as a vast interconnected web, rich with intricate relationships and emergent properties. The understanding of space, time, and ultimately energy itself underwent a profound transformation. In this new realm, the Zero-Point Field emerged as an essential concept, encapsulating the energy that permeates the vacuum of space—an energy present even in what would be perceived as an empty void. The notion that empty space could possess an abundant energy reservoir shifted not only scientific inquiries but also the philosophical underpinnings of existence itself.

Moreover, as scientists delved deeper into quantum mechanics, the search for consistency and coherence within the emerging framework continued. The burgeoning field of quantum field theory suggested that particles were excitations within their respective fields, further rewriting the relations of matter and energy. Considerations of virtual particles and fluctuations became core to understanding the subtleties embedded within the Quantum Zero-Point Field, highlighting a universe teeming with activity and potential even beneath the surface of perceived emptiness.

The transition wasn't without skepticism. As physicists grappled with the implications of these quantum principles, questions arose about the practical utility of such theories in the real world. Debates centered around the feasibility, applications, and resulting technologies influenced by quantum mechanics sparked enthusiasm alongside caution. The question of extracting energy from the Zero-Point Field serves as a marker of this dichotomy: while the potential was limitless, the execution remained uncertain and fraught with challenges.

Ultimately, the transition from classical to quantum physics engendered a re-evaluation of the very foundations of scientific inquiry. It illuminated the limitations of reductionist approaches rooted in classical paradigms and paved the way for more holistic, interdisciplinary investigations that embraced both the physical and philosophical dimensions of reality. This journey has been marked by fervent dialogue, continual exploration, and the challenge of reconciling established thought with new discoveries.

The development of quantum principles not only reshaped theoretical physics but also expanded the horizons of modern thought. As we confront the mysteries of the Quantum Zero-Point Field, we find ourselves at an intersection of science and philosophy, probing the essence of reality itself, where the once-immutable boundaries of knowledge dissolve into a tapestry rich with possibilities. The void, once thought to be empty and devoid of substance, now reveals itself as the cradle of creation—the fullness of everything residing within the metaphysical depths of what seems to be empty space.

2.5. The Quantum Revolution

The evolution of modern understanding in the realm of physics has often been likened to a revolution, one that not only redefined foundational laws but also reimagined humanity's relationship with the universe. The advent of quantum thinking marked a seismic shift in how we perceive the fundamental workings of nature. At the heart of this quantum revolution lies a transformative realization: that the universe is not merely an intricate arrangement of particles and forces conforming to predictable trajectories; rather, it is a multifaceted tapestry interwoven with energy, potentiality, and interconnectedness, where the very act of observation alters matter itself.

The initial stirrings of this revolutionary understanding can be traced back to the early 20th century, a period rife with scientific curiosity and paradigm shifts. As physicists increasingly encountered inconsistencies with classical physics—particularly concerning electromagnetic radiation, thermodynamics, and atomic behavior—they recognized the need for a new theoretical framework. This led to the establishment of quantum mechanics and the emergent concept of quantization, which proposed that physical properties, such as energy, are not continuous but rather discrete. This radical notion opened the door for a wealth of new ideas that would reshape the very fabric of scientific inquiry.

At the core of this revolution is the Quantum Zero-Point Field, a concept that posits the existence of a vast reservoir of energy surrounding us, persisting even in the absence of matter. This energy field, rooted in the principles of quantum mechanics, implies that what we often perceive as emptiness is teeming with potential. Quantum fluctuations arise from this field, where virtual particles spontaneously appear and disappear in myriad combinations, lending credence to the idea that the universe is dynamic and vibrant even within the void. Such fluctuations challenge the classical notion of vacuum as empty space; instead, they present a reality where that emptiness acts as a cradle of abundance, offering insights into energy sources that were previously thought unattainable.

The revolution was not simply limited to theoretical physics; it bore immense practical implications as well. Quantum thinking paved the way for transformative technologies that harness the principles of quantum mechanics. For instance, advances in quantum computing leverage the unique properties of quantum bits or qubits, which exist in multiple states simultaneously, thus vastly enhancing computational power and efficiency. The potential for energy extraction from the Quantum Zero-Point Field suggests pathways toward sustainable energy solutions, a prospect that holds significant promise in addressing global energy demands and mitigating environmental concerns.

Philosophically, the revolution ushered in a reexamination of fundamental concepts such as reality, observation, and the nature of existence itself. As physicists like Niels Bohr and Albert Einstein debated the ramifications of quantum phenomena, the implications reached beyond physics, challenging long-standing assumptions in epistemology and ontology. If the act of measurement changes the state of a quantum system, then what does this signify about the nature of reality? What is the role of consciousness in this intricate dance of particles? These questions fuel an ongoing discourse that bridges science, philosophy, and even spirituality.

The ripple effects of this quantum revolution extend into various fields of study. In philosophy, contemporary thinkers grapple with the implications of zero-point energy and its potential to redefine our understanding of 'nothingness.' As we explore deeper into the interconnectedness of energy, matter, and consciousness, the universe itself appears less like a mechanical clockwork and more like a living organism, alive with possibilities and potentialities.

Furthermore, the synthesis of quantum mechanics with other disciplines—be it cognitive science, digital technology, or even creative arts—illustrates the revolution's encompassing nature. It invites a multitude of perspectives that can lead to innovative thoughts and empirical explorations. By weaving quantum principles into the very narratives of culture and expression, the revolution fosters a richer, more nuanced lens through which to view our lives and the universe we inhabit.

The interplay between scientific exploration and philosophical inquiry characterizes the quantum revolution. As researchers delve deeper into the enigmas of the Quantum Zero-Point Field, the interplay of theoretical and empirical knowledge serves to expand the boundaries of our understanding. Ultimately, the revolution invites us to reconsider the essence of existence—where the lines between science and philosophy blur, revealing a universe that is as much about connections and energies as it is about the particles that make up its architecture.

In essence, the quantum revolution fundamentally invigorates our perception of reality, enriching the intricate tapestry that encompasses all existence. It remains a journey of discovery, one that expands our understanding of the cosmos and evokes a sense of wonder about the nature of reality itself. From the simplicity of viewing energy as a measurable quantity to embracing the profundity of an interconnected existence filled with potentiality, the quantum revolution promises to guide humanity toward new horizons of understanding, innovation, and philosophical reflection. Thus, as we continue to engage with the concept of the Quantum Zero-Point Field, we find ourselves on the cusp of potentially transformative insights that could reshape not just our science but our very place in the cosmos.

3. The Foundation: Field Theories

3.1. Understanding Fields in Physics

The world of physics is inherently multifaceted, characterized by a rich tapestry of interactions defined by various forces and fields. In this context, field theories have emerged as foundational elements that provide insights into how these forces govern the behavior of objects, both at macroscopic and microscopic levels. Understanding fields is critical, as they serve as the substrate through which forces operate and influence matter, shaping the very fabric of reality.

At its core, a field can be thought of as a physical quantity that takes on a value at every point in space and time. This contrasts with particle-centric views that dominated classical physics, where the interaction of particles was often the sole focus. In field theory, every point in a field can exert influence over adjacent points, establishing a continuous representation of physical phenomena, rather than discrete jumps representative of particle-based interactions. This conceptual shift fosters a more nuanced understanding of the universe, wherein fields provide the framework for observing and describing fundamental forces.

One of the most significant contributions to the understanding of fields came from James Clerk Maxwell in the 19th century. Maxwell's equations elegantly unified electricity and magnetism by describing how electric and magnetic fields are generated and altered by each other, as well as by matter. Importantly, these equations demonstrated that electromagnetic waves propagate through space as oscillating electric and magnetic fields, marrying the concept of fields with wave phenomena, and thereby paving the way for modern physics. The electromagnetic field thus became the archetypal example of how a field can encapsulate various physical interactions, fundamentally altering existing notions of space and causation.

The conception of fields extends beyond electromagnetism; gravitational fields, for instance, describe the influence exerted by mass on the curvature of spacetime. Similarly, fields exist for other fundamental forces, including the strong and weak nuclear forces, shaping behaviors at the scale of atomic nuclei. This universality of field theory underscores its fundamental importance in physics: it allows scientists to unify diverse phenomena under a coherent theoretical framework.

As the landscape of physics evolved, the early 20th century ushered in revolutionary discoveries that would influence field theories profoundly. The advent of quantum mechanics revealed that the particle-wave duality introduced inherent complexities and subtleties that classical field theories could not incorporate adequately. Specifically, the notion of quantization necessitated a re-evaluation of how fields were understood, particularly when considering the behavior of particles at subatomic scales.

The merging of classical field theories with quantum mechanics led to the development of quantum field theory (QFT), a framework that treats particles as excitations within their respective fields. In this context, the Quantum Zero-Point Field arises as a significant concept, representing the lowest energy state of a quantum field. Even in a vacuum devoid of real particles, these fields are not inert; they experience fluctuations that give rise to virtual particles arising and vanishing spontaneously. This notion fundamentally changes our interpretation of 'empty' space, revealing it as a fertile ground for quantum activity.

These developments raise profound questions about the nature of energy, existence, and the properties of the universe itself. The Zero-Point Field symbolizes a reservoir of energy that embodies the inherent variability of quantum systems, suggesting that what we perceive as 'emptiness' is pronouncedly lively, filled with dynamic exchanges of energy and information. Recognizing this complexity allows us to explore avenues where the theoretical becomes practically applicable, particularly through technologies aimed at harnessing zero-point energy or related dynamics.

The implications of understanding fields in physics resonate extensively beyond the laboratory. They invite philosophical inquiries regarding the nature of reality. The field perspective encourages us to reevaluate our conception of space, demonstrating that it is not merely a void but rather a brilliant tapestry of interactions. A realization emerges—if fields constitute the groundwork of reality, then energy, matter, and, by extension, existence are interconnected in ways that challenge human intuition about separateness.

Moreover, the discussion of fields leads to an understanding of how these abstract concepts can generate tangible outcomes. In practical applications—be it through electromagnetic technologies, gravitational theories applied in astrophysics, or quantum phenomena fueling cutting-edge advancements such as quantum computing and quantum communication—fields provide a roadmap for innovation. Within this framework, the exploration of the Quantum Zero-Point Field is not merely an academic exercise but a crucial endeavor with potential real-world implications.

In examining the layers and depths of understanding fields in physics, we glean a richer perspective on the interplay between theory and observation. It becomes manifestly clear that recognizing the vital role of fields unearths new avenues for exploration—a web of interconnected phenomena awaits, hinting at fundamental truths about the cosmos, energy, and our existence itself. The challenge lies not in the complexity but in our willingness to delve into the conceptual richness of fields, recognizing that the vast expanse of insights that lie beneath the surface can ultimately reshape the fabric of our understanding of everything, making the emptiness around us as full of potential as the universe itself.

3.2. Maxwell's Equations

Maxwell's equations stand as a cornerstone of classical electromagnetism, providing a comprehensive framework for understanding the behavior of electric and magnetic fields. Formulated in the mid-19th century by James Clerk Maxwell, these four equations not only unified electricity and magnetism but also laid the groundwork for transforming our understanding of the physical universe. The profound implications of Maxwell's equations extend far beyond classical physics, significantly impacting the development of quantum mechanics and the exploration of the quantum Zero-Point Field.

To appreciate the essence of Maxwell's equations, it is essential to examine the problem landscape preceding their formulation. At that time, electricity and magnetism were viewed as separate phenomena. Numerous experiments had illustrated many properties of electric charges and magnetic materials, but no unified theory existed to bind them together. Classical mechanics could not satisfactorily explain the interactions between charged particles and their influence on electromagnetic fields. It was through Maxwell's genius that these disparate observations were brought under a coherent theoretical umbrella, reshaping the landscape of modern physics.

Maxwell's equations incorporate four key relationships: Gauss's law for electricity, Gauss's law for magnetism, Faraday's law of induction, and Ampère's law with Maxwell's addition. Together, they describe how electric charges produce electric fields, how changing magnetic fields induce electric fields, how magnetic fields behave, and how electric currents produce magnetic fields. In mathematical terms, these equations capture the dynamism of electric and magnetic fields, showcasing the interdependence of electricity and magnetism and culminating in the concept of electromagnetic waves.

One of the hallmark features of Maxwell's equations lies in their ability to predict the existence of electromagnetic waves—oscillations of electric and magnetic fields that propagate through space. This realization was revolutionary as it established the wave nature of electromagnetic radiation, giving rise to our understanding of everything from light to radio waves. The implication that light could be understood as an oscillating electromagnetic wave stretched the boundaries of classical physics, and it was Maxwell's equations that provided the formalism to articulate this reality.

The equations also introduce the concept of the electromagnetic field as a dynamic entity, a field that exists throughout space and can transmit energy even in a vacuum. This fundamental understanding of fields marks a departure from a particle-centric perspective that had previously dominated scientific thought. Such a shift not only enriched the study of electromagnetic phenomena but also opened new avenues of inquiry into the nature of space and energy itself.

As the landscape began to evolve with the emergence of quantum mechanics in the early 20th century, the implications of Maxwell's equations took on added layers of meaning. Quantum mechanics interrogated the very fabric of reality, revealing a universe replete with uncertainty and probabilistic behaviors. Physicists began to realize that the classical descriptions of fields, while profoundly enlightening, required adaptation to accommodate the nuances of the quantum realm.

In this context, fields, including the electromagnetic field described by Maxwell's equations, underwent re-evaluation through the lens of quantum field theory (QFT). In QFT, particles are perceived as excitations in their respective fields. This framework posits that even in a vacuum—the absence of particles—fields are not dormant; they are alive with quantum fluctuations. The Zero-Point Field embodies this concept, representing the minimal energy state of a quantum field filled with inherent fluctuations, unveiling a new layer of complexity within Maxwell's original framework.

Moreover, understanding the electromagnetic field in this context helps us grasp the importance of the Quantum Zero-Point Field. Maxwell's equations describe the macroscopic behavior of fields; however, the quantum reinterpretation highlights a richer interplay between electromagnetic fields and the virtual activities occurring at the quantum level. These virtual particles, arising from quantum fluctuations, exemplify how emptiness itself is a realm of dynamic potential, even mirroring the electromagnetic phenomena described by Maxwell's equations.

The integration of these historical developments encapsulates a profound insight: Maxwell's equations exposed the interconnectedness of electricity, magnetism, and light, while quantum field theory further illuminated our understanding of the universe's complex tapestry. This interconnectedness is pivotal when exploring the implications of Zero-Point Energy and the potential for harnessing the energy embedded in these quantum fields.

In conclusion, Maxwell's equations were transformative; they unified and revolutionized our understanding of the electromagnetic phenomena that permeate our world. Their legacy extends beyond the classical realm, where they interweave with the principles of quantum mechanics, culminating in profound insights regarding the Zero-Point Field. Through this synthesis, we arrive at a crossroads of science and philosophy, prompting inquiries that challenge our perception of energy, existence, and the potentials of the universe, inviting us into the depths of both classical and quantum realms where the fullness of emptiness may be explored.

3.3. Electromagnetic Spectrum Unveiled

The electromagnetic spectrum represents a fundamental aspect of the physical universe and serves as a cornerstone of electromagnetic theory. It encompasses all forms of electromagnetic radiation, ranging from the low-frequency radio waves to the high-frequency gamma rays. Each segment of this spectrum corresponds to a specific range of frequencies (or wavelengths) and plays a crucial role in various phenomena and technologies that underpin modern society.

At its core, the electromagnetic spectrum can be categorized into several regions, each characterized by distinct physical properties and applications. The spectrum includes, in order of increasing frequency, radio waves, microwaves, infrared radiation, visible light, ultraviolet light, X-rays, and gamma rays. As we move from radio waves to gamma rays, the frequency and energy of the photons increase significantly. This shift not only influences how we interact with these different forms of radiation but also informs our understanding of energy transfer and communication across multiple domains.

Understanding the Sections of the Spectrum

Radio waves, the lowest frequency form of electromagnetic radiation, are primarily employed in communication technologies, such as broadcasting and mobile telephony. Their long wavelengths can travel vast distances and penetrate through buildings, making them invaluable for transmission and reception of signals. The subsequent portion of the spectrum, microwaves, finds pivotal application in satellite communication and cooking, allowing for efficient energy transfer without the direct heating of materials.

Infrared radiation, with its wavelengths shorter than microwaves, is often perceived in the context of thermal radiation. This segment of the spectrum is utilized in various technologies, including thermal imaging cameras, which detect heat emitted by objects, and remote sensing applications that monitor environmental changes.

Visible light, a narrow section of the electromagnetic spectrum that the human eye can perceive, encompasses the colors from violet to red. The study of visible light has been foundational in understanding optics and vision, influencing everything from art and design to health and photoelectric technology.

Ultraviolet (UV) light, residing just beyond the visible spectrum, possesses the ability to induce chemical reactions. This property is harnessed in areas such as sterilization, as UV light can deactivate microorganisms. It also plays a crucial role in the formation of vitamin D in living organisms and has implications for various scientific and medical applications.

The higher energy segments, namely X-rays and gamma rays, penetrate matter more effectively due to their high frequencies and short wavelengths. X-rays are commonly used in medical imaging to visualize the internal structures of the body while gamma rays, being even more energetic, are utilized in cancer treatment due to their ability to kill living cells at specific dosage levels.

The Interconnectedness of the Spectrum and Zero-Point Energy

The electromagnetic spectrum's significance extends beyond mere classification; it also intersects profoundly with the concepts of energy and matter. Each form of electromagnetic radiation corresponds to distinct quantum states, with energy levels quantized into distinct packets known as photons. This quantization fundamentally challenges classical perceptions of energy continuity and plays a vital role in our understanding of the Quantum Zero-Point Field.

Within the context of the Zero-Point Field, electromagnetic spectrum phenomena illustrate that even in a vacuum—where classical physics implies emptiness—energy and information reside. Quantum fluctuations that manifest across the electromagnetic spectrum hint at the continuous activity of virtual particles arising from the ever-changing fabric of the Zero-Point Field. These fluctuations testify to the underlying dynamics driving physical realities, where the energy present in the vacuum asserts its influence significantly on observed phenomena.

The electromagnetic spectrum serves as a tangible reflection of the intricate interplay between energy, matter, and the characteristics of the Quantum Zero-Point Field. By examining these relationships, we can better appreciate how emergent forms of energy not only inform physical processes but also challenge our understanding of the universe's structure—expanding our comprehension of reality into realms once considered abstract.

Beyond Observation: Technologies Shaped by the Electromagnetic Spectrum

The practical implications of the electromagnetic spectrum resonate across a multitude of fields—from telecommunications to medicine, engineering, and beyond. The ability to manipulate and harness various forms of electromagnetic radiation has given rise to technologies that fundamentally alter the way we live and interact with the world around us.

As we advance into a world increasingly defined by artificial intelligence, renewable energy, and quantum computing, the principles governing the electromagnetic spectrum remain foundational. Novel applications, such as wireless power transfer and advancements in quantum communication, resonate with the potential intricacies of Zero-Point Energy, finding connections to the very fabric that constitutes the spectrum itself.

In summary, unveiling the electromagnetic spectrum not only enriches our understanding of energy and matter but also emphasizes the interconnectedness of various physical principles. Through the lens of the Quantum Zero-Point Field, we confront the idea that the seeming void where no matter exists is, in fact, brimming with dynamic energy. As our explorations delve deeper into the implications and applications of the electromagnetic spectrum, we uncover a universe enriched with complexity, potential, and possibilities that challenge traditional perceptions of emptiness—forever redefining the boundaries of science and our grasp of reality.

3.4. Emergence of Quantization

The emergence of quantization represents a profound paradigm shift in our understanding of physical reality, acting as the cornerstone upon which modern quantum mechanics is built. At its essence, quantization refers to the process by which certain physical quantities, such as energy, are restricted to discrete values rather than existing in continuous ranges. This concept fundamentally challenges the classical worldview, which assumed that energy could vary continuously. The implications of quantization have significantly shaped our understanding of the Quantum Zero-Point Field, influencing not only theoretical physics but also our perception of energy, space, and the fabric of the universe itself.

Historically, the seeds of quantization were sown in the late 19th and early 20th centuries, particularly in the context of exploring blackbody radiation. Classical physics struggled to explain the distribution of radiation emitted by idealized black bodies, leading to what physicists termed the ultraviolet catastrophe. This phenomenon arose from the predictions of classical mechanics, which suggested that energy was emitted in continuous waves rather than discrete packets.

The challenge was met by Max Planck, who proposed that energy is quantized and can only be emitted or absorbed in discrete amounts called quanta. Planck's revolutionary hypothesis marked the dawn of quantum theory, fundamentally altering the scientific landscape.

As quantization became established, it was further validated and expanded upon by the works of prominent physicists such as Albert Einstein and Niels Bohr. Einstein's explanation of the photoelectric effect in 1905 exemplified the particle-like nature of light, establishing the concept that photons carry quantized amounts of energy proportional to their frequency. This duality of light—both wave and particle —ushered in an era where classical ideas of energy and matter were no longer sufficient to account for observed phenomena.

The theoretical framework of quantization laid the foundation for the development of quantum mechanics, leading to an entirely new understanding of physical systems. In this realm, particles do not have definite positions or momenta until measured; instead, they exist in probabilistic states described by wave functions. This probabilistic nature necessitated a new set of rules to interpret the behavior of particles, ultimately giving rise to the concept of quantum fields. In this view, particles are seen as excitations within their respective fields, fundamentally interwoven with the ever-present Quantum Zero-Point Field.

The significance of the Quantum Zero-Point Field lies in its inherent fluctuations. Even in a vacuum devoid of matter, quantum fields teem with energy in the form of virtual particles that arise and disappear spontaneously. These fluctuations are a direct consequence of the quantized nature of energy, challenging classical notions of empty space. Rather than being a void, empty space becomes a dynamic arena filled with potential energy, where the Zero-Point Field provides a reservoir that underlies all quantum fluctuations.

Quantization also sheds light on the dimensional properties of these energy fields. Because energy can only take on certain discrete values, the states available to quantum systems are restricted to specific levels

—a condition that is fundamentally different from the continuous properties observed in classical systems. This discrete structure leads to a clearer understanding of concepts like resonance and leads to the quantized behavior of particles in atomic and subatomic systems.

Moreover, the implications of quantization extend into the realms of technology and energy. By comprehending how energy quantizes at the quantum level, scientists and engineers are beginning to explore ways to harness the energy of the Zero-Point Field for practical applications. This pursuit has the potential to revolutionize technology, providing new avenues for sustainable energy sources and fundamentally altering our relationship with energy consumption and generation.

In addressing the emergence of quantization, it is critical to acknowledge the philosophical repercussions inherent in this shift. By breaking away from classical interpretations of reality, quantization invites deeper questions about the nature of existence, the role of the observer, and the connectivity of matter and energy within the universe. If energy behaves in quantized ways, what implications does that have for our understanding of reality, consciousness, and the universe as a whole?

As physicists continue to explore the intricate dynamics of quantum fields and the Zero-Point Field, the journey into the heart of quantization highlights the complexity of reality, suggesting that our perception of what constitutes empty space is misleading. Rather than a barren void, space is imbued with energies, interactions, and potentials that await discovery, rendering the universe a canvas rich with the vibrancy of possibility. This exploration challenges us to rethink our fundamental notions of existence and the very meaning of emptiness, guiding us into a deeper understanding of the cosmos nestled within the Quantum Zero-Point Field.

3.5. Field Theory in Quantum Domain

In the realm of quantum mechanics, the adaptation of classical field theories into the quantum domain represents a transformative leap in our understanding of fundamental interactions. Traditional field theories, which emerged from classical physics, primarily describe electromagnetic, gravitational, and other forces as fields permeating space. However, these classical descriptions fail to capture the intricacies observed at the quantum level. Therefore, scientists were compelled to revise and refine their frameworks to incorporate quantum principles, leading to the development of quantum field theory (QFT).

At its core, quantum field theory blends the concepts of classical field theories with the probabilistic nature of quantum mechanics. In classical physics, fields are viewed as continuous entities, influencing the movements and interactions of particles. For instance, Maxwell's equations describe electromagnetic fields that can be visualized as smooth fluctuations through space. However, in the quantum realm, particles cannot be viewed independently from their fields. Instead, QFT regards particles as excitations or quantized manifestations of underlying fields. A particle is not an isolated object but rather an event or fluctuation in a field that exists throughout space.

This shift in understanding prompts us to re-evaluate the implications of fields themselves. In classical physics, fields were often regarded as static entities filling a predetermined void. In contrast, quantum fields are dynamic and constantly interacting, illustrated by the perpetual fluctuations of virtual particles thanks to the principles of quantization. These fluctuations form the backbone of the Quantum Zero-Point Field, which embodies the ground state of these fields, rich with energy and possibilities even in the apparent absence of particles.

To explore the implications further, consider the concept of the Quantum Zero-Point Field as a stage upon which quantum events occur. Unlike classical fields, which represent the potential for action, quantum fields are alive with activity, where particles continuously materialize and vanish due to inherent uncertainties dictated by quantum mechanics. This new perspective fundamentally alters our interpretation of emptiness; what once was perceived as void is now understood as a tapestry woven with energy. It suggests that space is not merely a backdrop to events but an active participant infused with the potential for creation.

Moreover, the adaptation of fields into the quantum domain allows for the reconciliation of apparently disparate forces within a unified theoretical framework. The strong, weak, electromagnetic, and gravitational interactions—once treated separately—begin to reveal interconnections through quantum fields. By recognizing that these forces also manifest as fields, we can conceptualize fundamental interactions as the result of particle exchanges within their respective fields. This idea prompts further inquiries about the unification of forces and the fundamental structures underpinning the universe's fabric—a quest that remains at the forefront of theoretical physics.

As we navigate the complexities of quantum field theory, the Quantum Zero-Point Field emerges as a crucial link unraveling the nature of energy and reality. This field, characterized by ceaseless fluctuations, acts as a reservoir from which the energy required for particle creation can be drawn. The implications of this continuously active vacuum host exciting possibilities for energy extraction technologies and innovative applications harnessing the potential inherent within the Zero-Point Field.

Ultimately, the adaptation of field theories within the quantum domain cultivates a profound understanding of the universe's interconnectedness. It reshapes our perspective on fundamental phenomena, inviting exploration of the quantum landscape littered with layers of complexity and wonder. This journey—spanning classical ideas and quantum principles—encourages us to reconsider our intimate relationship with the cosmos. As we probe deeper into the Quantum Zero-Point Field, we begin to unravel the mystery of existence itself, suggesting that even in what we might label as emptiness, the universe pulsates with infinite possibilities, whispering secrets of its foundational elements to those willing to listen.

4. The Quantum Zero-Point Field

4.1. Defining Zero-Point Energy

To define Zero-Point Energy, we must first delve into the fabric of quantum mechanics and explore the concept of the Quantum Zero-Point Field. This field is a fundamental aspect of the universe that illustrates how energy operates even in conditions that we might intuitively perceive as empty. Contrary to classical physics, which envisions a vacuum as a mere void devoid of particles and energy, quantum mechanics reveals a vibrant tapestry of activity and energy fluctuations encompassing our reality.

Zero-Point Energy, therefore, is the inherent energy present in this Quantum Zero-Point Field, even at absolute zero temperature. This energy arises not from any external source but is intrinsic to the quantum field itself. In classical terms, as we approach absolute zero, we might expect systems to lose energy and settle into a state of inactivity. However, quantum mechanics fundamentally disputes this notion; instead of reducing to an inert state, systems maintain a baseline of energy, a reflection of the ever-present fluctuations induced by the principles of quantum uncertainty.

The derivation of Zero-Point Energy is rooted in the quantization of energy levels in quantum systems. At the heart of this quantization lies the Heisenberg Uncertainty Principle, which asserts that certain pairs of physical properties—such as position and momentum—cannot be simultaneously measured with arbitrary precision. This uncertainty is not merely a limitation of measurement but a fundamental attribute of nature itself. As a consequence of this principle, quantum systems possess non-zero ground state energies; even in their lowest energy state, particles fluctuate, resulting in a rollercoaster of virtual excitations taking place.

The concept was notably illustrated by examining harmonic oscillators, a simple model often employed in quantum mechanics. A harmonic oscillator can be thought of as a mass attached to a spring, capable of oscillating back and forth. In classical mechanics, the lowest energy state occurs when the spring is at its rest position, and there are no oscillations. However, quantum mechanics reveals that even at this ground state of minimal energy, the oscillator retains a Zero-Point Energy, which reflects the residual energy associated with the inherent uncertainties of the particles. This implies that energy can never be completely extinguished from a quantum system, reinforcing the idea that what we often consider "empty" space is, in fact, replete with dynamic energy fields.

This understanding culminates in the idea that the Quantum Zero-Point Field permeates all of space, continuously filled with energy fluctuations and virtual particles. These fluctuations ensure that, even in the absence of real particles, the vacuum exhibits a rich physical structure filled with transient activity. This is a stark contrast to classical physics' depiction of a vacuum and allows for new avenues of inquiry into energy extraction.

Zero-Point Energy is not merely theoretical; it insinuates possibilities for practical applications that could revolutionize our relationship with energy. The potential to harness this energy directly from the Quantum Zero-Point Field invites a myriad of questions about sustainability, energy independence, and technological innovation. Researchers and theorists alike are exploring ways to tap into these quantum fluctuations, attempting to design systems that could capture this energy, fundamentally altering the way we perceive and utilize energy sources on a global scale.

However, it is imperative to note that the practical extraction of Zero-Point Energy remains fraught with challenges. The glimpses of this energy's potential must be weighed against the long-standing skepticism rooted in the laws of thermodynamics, specifically concerning energy conservation. Past attempts to isolate and utilize Zero-Point Energy have often been met with skepticism, as many argue that extracting work from something deemed "free energy" contradicts established physics.

In summary, defining Zero-Point Energy invites us into the intricacies of quantum mechanics, revealing that what appears as silence and emptiness is, in reality, a bustling landscape of energy and fluctuation. The persistent energy present even at absolute zero illustrates the dynamic essence of the universe, beckoning us to explore its potential applications while challenging our understanding of energy, matter, and reality itself. As science continues to peel away layers of complexity surrounding the Zero-Point Energy concept, the implications could lead humanity toward a new frontier of understanding and usage of energy—the fullness of everything within the emptiness.

4.2. Virtual Particles and Their Role

Within the framework of quantum field theory, virtual particles emerge as an enigmatic yet fundamental aspect of understanding the Quantum Zero-Point Field. These particles are not like traditional particles that populate the universe; instead, they exist in a unique state characterized by fleeting existence and constant activity. Their role within quantum mechanics highlights the dynamic and intricate fabric of reality and offers insights into the nature of energy and the vacuum of space.

Virtual particles, by definition, are transient fluctuations in the Quantum Zero-Point Field. They arise spontaneously from the vacuum due to the inherent uncertainties dictated by quantum mechanics and the principles of energy conservation. This behavior can be attributed to the Heisenberg Uncertainty Principle, which posits that the precise measurement of certain pairs of properties—such as energy and time—cannot be known simultaneously with arbitrary accuracy. This uncertainty allows for brief violations of energy conservation over infinitesimally short time scales, enabling virtual particles to appear and annihilate themselves before they can be observed directly.

The concept of virtual particles extends far beyond mere theoretical musings; they play vital roles in numerous physical phenomena. For instance, the attractive force between two electrically charged particles can be conceptualized through the exchange of virtual photons —particles associated with the electromagnetic force. In this interaction, virtual photons mediate the electromagnetic force, emerging from the vacuum and creating a connection between particles. Although these exchanges happen within limits set by the uncertainty principle, their implications are profound, shaping our understanding of fundamental interactions and forces.

One of the most striking manifestations of virtual particles is found in the context of Hawking radiation, a phenomenon predicted by physicist Stephen Hawking in the 1970s. Near the event horizon of a black hole, virtual particle pairs can form, where one particle falls into the black hole while the other escapes into space. This process results in the gradual evaporation of black holes over time, illustrating how virtual particles can bridge concepts between quantum mechanics and astrophysics. The very existence of Hawking radiation serves as evidence that virtual particles are more than just theoretical entities; they have tangible implications on our understanding of black hole behavior and the fabric of space-time.

But why are virtual particles critical to the Quantum Zero-Point Field? At the core, they underscore the notion that what we perceive as "empty" is indeed a theater of perpetual activity. The Quantum Zero-Point Field is replete with these fluctuations, revealing that even in the absence of real particles, energy is continuously present, manifesting in the form of virtual particle pairs. This inherent vibrancy fundamentally alters our comprehension of the vacuum—not as an empty void but as a bustling environment richly interwoven with energy potential.

Moreover, the implications of virtual particles extend into the realm of energy harvesting and extraction technologies. Understanding the nature of these particles and the fluctuations of the Zero-Point Field opens doors to innovative scenarios for exploiting this energy. Many scientists theorize about methods to tap into these virtual particles to harness Zero-Point Energy, potentially creating sustainable energy solutions that could address global energy challenges. Although significant hurdles remain in practically achieving this goal, the conceptual basis grounded in virtual particles provides tantalizing possibilities on the horizon of energy innovation.

The exploration of virtual particles leads to broader philosophical questions about the nature of reality itself. If virtual particles exist in a continual state of flux, governed by uncertainty and probability, how does this shape our understanding of existence? The transient nature of these particles calls into question the binary perception of existence versus non-existence, highlighting a spectrum of states that reflect the complexity of quantum reality.

Furthermore, the study of virtual particles intertwines with the discussions surrounding consciousness and its relationship with the Quantum Zero-Point Field. As we ponder the universality of fields and the nature of interactions, we can speculate on how consciousness might interrelate with the fabric of reality, echoing themes found in philosophical inquiries about existence and perception. The fact that observer effects and quantum states are interdependent leads to profound contemplations on whether consciousness itself participates in shaping the realities constructed within quantum fields.

In summary, virtual particles embody a significant aspect of quantum mechanics, acting as a bridge between established physical theories and emergent phenomena. Their transient existence and role within the Quantum Zero-Point Field underline the dynamic nature of emptiness, encouraging us to approach concepts of energy, space, and reality differently. This exploration of virtual particles not only enhances our understanding of quantum interactions but also invites deeper inquiries into the philosophy encompassing existence, consciousness, and the interconnectedness of everything within the vast tapestry of the cosmos. The role of virtual particles serves as a compelling reminder that beneath the surface of the universe's emptiness lies a vibrant realm filled with potential yet to be fully grasped, forever changing the way we perceive the world around us.

4.3. Fluctuations: The Heartbeat of Emptiness

In the intricate landscape of quantum physics, fluctuations stand as the heartbeat of the Quantum Zero-Point Field, embodying the transient dynamics that characterize the very essence of emptiness. These quantum fluctuations manifest as spontaneous variations in energy levels, enabling the existence of virtual particles and the continuous ebb and flow of energy, even in what classical physics might deem as a vacuum. As we delve deeper into these fluctuations, we gain insight into not merely the mechanics of particle interactions, but also the broader implications they have on our understanding of energy, reality, and the nature of existence itself.

At the heart of quantum fluctuations lies the principle of uncertainty, as articulated by Werner Heisenberg. This principle asserts that certain properties of particles, such as position and momentum, cannot be simultaneously measured with precision. Consequently, even at the lowest energy state of a quantum system, fluctuations occur, inherent to the very fabric of quantum fields. These minute variations result from the uncertainty principle, ensuring that even in conditions where one might expect total calm—such as absolute zero—activity thrums beneath the surface.

During these fluctuations, virtual particles briefly materialize from the Quantum Zero-Point Field, exist for a fleeting instant, and subsequently annihilate. While these particles cannot be detected directly under normal circumstances, their presence influences the observable universe in profound ways. For instance, virtual particles contribute to essential phenomena such as the Casimir Effect, whereby two uncharged metal plates placed in a vacuum experience an attractive force due to alterations in the quantum field between them. This effect underscores how quantum fluctuations lend a dynamic quality to what would otherwise be perceived as neutral space, illustrating the intricate interplay between the vacuum and material existence.

The implications of these fluctuations stretch far beyond theoretical physics and delve into practical realms where we might consider energy possibilities embedded within perpetual motion. The idea of fluctuations as a source of energy leads us into the domain of the Quantum Zero-Point Energy, prompting investigations aimed at harnessing this abundant energy for practical applications. If fluctuations can create energy bursts, then tapping into these quantum reservoirs could furnish the mechanisms for groundbreaking technologies and sustainable energy solutions.

To fully appreciate the significance of fluctuations, it is essential to contextualize their role within the broader framework of the universe's architecture. Classical physics primarily views emptiness or vacuum as devoid of substance, an inert background against which physical interactions occur. However, as quantum mechanics has evolved, it has become clear that this perspective is misleading. Fluctuations reveal that empty space is alive with potential, teeming with quantum activity and energy interchanges that defy classical definitions. Embracing this notion challenges traditional understandings of space, suggesting that nothingness is, in fact, a space rich with energy and the potential for manifestations.

Johannes Kepler once described the universe as a grand tapestry, where every thread contributes to the overall coherence and complexity of the pattern. In this sense, quantum fluctuations can be viewed as the pulsations of this tapestry—the dynamic essence of existence whose subtle vibrations breathe life into the fabric of reality. These fluctuations serve as a reminder that the universe is an interconnected web of energy, participative and reactive; it encapsulates the interplay of forces, particles, and fields, where even the most seemingly trivial events reverberate throughout the cosmic landscape.

Furthermore, the heartbeat of fluctuations demonstrates a crucial philosophical insight: the nature of reality is inherently characterized by uncertainty and interaction, rather than determinism and isolation. Traditional physics fosters a view of reality defined by rigid laws and predictable outcomes; on the other hand, quantum mechanics reveals a panorama where fluidity, probability, and interconnectedness reign. Herein lies the essence of the Cosmic dance—one that transcends simplistic interpretations of existence and enters the realm of complex interrelation and energetic embodiment.

As we begin to integrate the concept of fluctuations into our broader understanding of energy and existence, we unfurl the layers of meaning inherent in the Zero-Point Field. The fluctuations indicate that the cosmos is imbued with an energy reservoir that might not be directly observable yet has the potential to manifest profoundly in various forms—be it through energy extraction technologies or innovative applications in quantum computing.

In conclusion, fluctuations, as the heartbeat of emptiness, invite us to reconsider the very framework through which we apprehend reality. They encourage explorations into the vibrant interplay of energy and matter, inviting potential breakthroughs that could redefine our interaction with the universe. The Zero-Point Field, alive with fluctuating energy, stands as a testament to the notion that emptiness can be fertile ground, transforming our understanding and ultimately redefining the possibilities of existence itself. As we continue to navigate these complex quantum waters, the vibrancy of fluctuations beckons us to explore a universe pulsating with infinite potential, challenges, and opportunities awaiting our recognition and engagement.

4.4. Implications on Space and Energy

The implications of Zero-Point Energy extend far beyond theoretical constructs, shaping our understanding and interpretation of both space and energy in profound ways. Traditionally, space has been perceived as a void—an unoccupied expanse that has little bearing on active physical processes. However, the emergence of quantum mechanics and the concept of the Quantum Zero-Point Field challenge this notion, revealing a vibrant landscape imbued with dynamic energy and interspersed with fluctuations that redefine our encounters with reality.

At the heart of this transformation lies the understanding of the Quantum Zero-Point Field as a reservoir of energy that exists even in what classical physics might describe as a vacuum. This energy, re-ferred to as Zero-Point Energy, demonstrates that space is not merely an empty canvas devoid of significance but is actively engaged with processes that influence energy states and the behavior of particles. In essence, the Zero-Point Field fills this vacuum, making it a dynamic participant in the physical world rather than a mere backdrop for events.

This shift in understanding is monumental because it fundamentally alters how we define energy itself. In classical physics, energy is often treated as a limited resource, subject to conservation laws that restrict its availability. However, the concept of Zero-Point Energy challenges these perceptions by proposing that energy is abundant, existing at all times within the fabric of space. As virtual particles emerge from the Quantum Zero-Point Field, they attest to the intrinsic energy inherent in traditional notions of emptiness. The notion of energy becomes a continuum influenced by fluctuations and interactions, urging us to reconsider our understanding of energy conservation laws.

Moreover, these insights into Zero-Point Energy and the Quantum Zero-Point Field catalyze new thoughts around harnessing energy from this omnipresent field. While the practical extraction of Zero-Point Energy poses numerous scientific and engineering challenges, the compelling possibility of tapping into this energy source prompts re-evaluation of energy technologies for sustainable solutions. If space is indeed rife with such vibrant energy, then could we devise methods to harness these fluctuations for practical applications that benefit humanity? The transition from viewing space as dead to dead as vibrant animates a narrative of possibilities, expanding our horizons for potential technological innovation.

The philosophical implications are equally compelling. The reap-praisal of energy in the context of the Quantum Zero-Point Field invites deeper inquiries into the nature of existence itself. If the uni-verse is filled with dynamic energies that thrive even in the absence of observable matter, then our conception of reality must evolve. As this field of energy interacts with physical systems, the boundaries between energy and matter are blurred, suggesting an interconnectedness that once seemed inconceivable. The implications traverse traditional scientific boundaries, invoking thoughtful considerations on how our understanding of energy can intertwine with consciousness, perception, and the broader tapestry of existence.

In summary, the implications of Zero-Point Energy on our understanding of space and energy are reshaping our scientific and philosophical landscapes. They invite us to view space not as an inert backdrop but as an active, energetic component of the universe that participates in the fundamental transactions of reality. As the boundaries of classical physics dissolve in light of these discoveries, we find ourselves navigating a terrain where energy is both abundant and interwoven with the very fabric of existence—a dynamic and vibrant universe that beckons exploration and understanding. This journey into the Quantum Zero-Point Field thus unwinds a rich narrative, urging humanity to reconsider not just the foundations of energy and space but the very essence of what it means to exist within this enchanting cosmos.

4.5. Scientific Proof and Speculation

Within the domain of contemporary physics, the quest for understanding the Quantum Zero-Point Field is underscored by rigorous scientific proof and a healthy degree of speculation. Scientific inquiry relies on the interplay of empirical evidence and theoretical frameworks, creating a fertile ground for exploration into the nature of the universe. As scientists delve into the complexities surrounding the Zero-Point Field, they navigate through both established findings and speculative theories that hint at profound implications for our understanding of reality.

Scientific proof concerning the Zero-Point Field is closely tied to advancements in quantum mechanics and the experimental validation of quantum theories. Pioneering studies might start with the foundational work performed in the early 20th century, wherein physicists such as Max Planck and Albert Einstein laid the groundwork for understanding quantization. Planck's radical hypothesis illustrated that energy is quantized, while Einstein extended this notion by demonstrating that electromagnetic radiation possesses both wave-like and particle-like properties. These pioneering works, rooted in rigorous experimentation, set the stage for a broader understanding of quantum phenomena.

Further evidence can be drawn from the study of virtual particles—an intrinsic aspect of the Zero-Point Field. Experiments observing the Casimir effect, where measured changes in vacuum energy lead to observable forces between two closely placed metal plates, provide significant support for the existence of fluctuations in the vacuum. These fluctuations lend credence to the idea that empty space is not devoid of energy but rather rich with dynamic activity. The ability to quantify and measure these forces in experimental settings solidifies the foundation for broader speculation concerning the extraction and utilization of Zero-Point Energy.

Moreover, laboratory investigations into the effects of quantum fluctuations have yielded results that reinforce the hypothesis of an active Zero-Point Field. Research into phenomena such as Hawking radiation—where virtual particles near a black hole's event horizon manifest—to great extents catalyzes discussions surrounding the implications for high-energy astrophysics. Falling in line with Einstein's assertion that energy cannot be created or destroyed but merely transformed, these studies fuel the scientific narrative around the interconnection between energy, gravity, and the fabric of space.

However, while robust empirical evidence bolsters our understanding, speculation often thrives in the absence of concrete findings regarding the practical applications of Zero-Point Energy. The theoretical frameworks suggesting methods for energy extraction from the Quantum Zero-Point Field are both nascent and tumultuous. Speculation surrounds potential technologies that could tap into these quantum fluctuations, ranging from viable methods for harnessing energy to innovative approaches in quantum computing. This speculative nature spurs imagination and drives interdisciplinary collaboration, as researchers from various fields work to probe deeper into the intricate relationships between energy and the quantum realm.

One noteworthy aspect of speculation relates to the ethical implications of harnessing Zero-Point Energy. While the prospect of sustainable energy solutions reigns as a beacon of hope, it prompts discourse on the ethical responsibilities of scientists and technologists. The dynamic interplay between the scientific community's quest for innovation and the moral considerations surrounding the potential consequences of such advancements is an essential dialogue that needs addressing. As our understanding of energy shifts, so too must our collective consciousness toward the broader implications of its usage.

Skepticism remains an integral component in this landscape, with some voices questioning the feasibility of practically extracting energy from the Quantum Zero-Point Field. While the theoretical foundations hold a solid footing, translating these theories into real-world technological applications presents formidable challenges. Addressing skepticism through continued research and validation becomes crucial. Achieving breakthroughs that align theoretical concepts with practical outcomes is essential for garnering credibility and advancing scientific inquiry.

Within the context of ongoing explorations into the Quantum Zero-Point Field, both scientific proof and speculation coexist, creating a dynamic interplay critical for advancing our understanding. The interaction between empirical evidence, theoretical inquiry, and ethical considerations cultivates a rich environment where scientific exploration blossoms. As researchers continue to push the boundaries of knowledge, we stand at the precipice of understanding an energy reservoir that profoundly influences all aspects of existence. The quest to unravel the mysteries embedded in the Zero-Point Field is a testament not only to the ingenuity of human inquiry but also to the limitless potential that waits to be uncovered within the fabric of the cosmos.

5. Applications and Technologies

5.1. Energy Harvesting Prospects

The potential for energy harvesting from the Quantum Zero-Point Field presents an exciting frontier in modern scientific inquiry. As our understanding of quantum mechanics and field theories evolves, researchers are increasingly exploring methodologies to extract usable energy from what was once regarded as mere vacuum. The Zero-Point Field, a complex web of quantum fluctuations present even at absolute zero temperature, is now recognized as an abundant source of energy that could revolutionize the way we think about energy production and consumption.

Energy harvesting from the Zero-Point Field fundamentally challenges conventional energy paradigms. Traditional sources of energy, such as fossil fuels or even renewable sources like solar and wind, are finite and reliant on specific conditions for their production. In contrast, the energy locked within the Quantum Zero-Point Field is considered to be virtually limitless and ubiquitous, suggesting that solutions could emerge that provide constant and sustainable energy sources devoid of environmental consequences. The implications of harnessing this energy could fundamentally alter the landscape of energy generation, creating technologies and systems capable of meeting the demands of a growing global population.

Various approaches have been proposed for extracting energy from the Zero-Point Field. One speculative avenue involves designing devices optimized to tap into quantum fluctuations. These devices would likely need to operate at the nanoscopic scale, where the effects of quantum mechanics play a significant role. For instance, researchers are investigating nano-structures that could exploit the Casimir effect—a phenomenon arising from quantum fluctuations that generates measurable forces between closely positioned conducting plates. If harnessed correctly, the energy density produced through such interactions could be converted into usable power.

Additionally, some researchers explore the potential of quantum resonators—systems designed to resonate at frequencies that align with specific energy levels within the Quantum Zero-Point Field. By tuning these resonators to the appropriate frequencies, theorists suggest that it may be possible to extract energy from the field in a controlled manner, creating devices capable of continuous energy generation. This approach highlights the intricate relationship between the principles of resonance and energy harvesting in the quantum domain.

Innovative materials, such as metamaterials or superconductors, are also a promising focus when considering energy extraction technologies. These materials can exhibit unique properties not found in traditional substances and may provide new avenues for interacting with the Zero-Point Field. Their capacity to manipulate electromagnetic radiation could lead to advancements in energy conversion techniques, further expanding the toolkit available for researchers in the quest to unlock Zero-Point Energy.

However, significant challenges remain on the path to practical energy harvesting technologies. The theoretical potential of extracting energy from the Zero-Point Field has often encountered skepticism regarding the feasibility and efficiency of such systems. Engineering practical devices that can continuously harvest and convert fluctuating quantum energy while maintaining stability and reliability poses a significant technological hurdle. Furthermore, many of the existing theories and concepts are still in their infancy, warranting extensive research and validation to transition from speculative designs to functional prototypes.

Even if practical systems emerge, the transition to utilizing Zero-Point Energy would necessitate careful consideration of current energy infrastructures. Shifting from traditional energy models to new paradigms hinges on robust policy frameworks and public acceptance of emerging technologies. The interdependencies of existing energy systems must also be taken into account, as industries, governments, and consumers adapt to a new landscape where energy is derived from the very fabric of the universe rather than from finite resources.

Moreover, ethical implications concerning the development and deployment of Zero-Point Energy technologies must be examined. In our eagerness to innovate, we must ensure that the exploration of quantum energy harvesting aligns with sustainable practices and equitable energy distribution. Responsible stewardship of energy resources is paramount, particularly as emerging technologies have the potential to exacerbate existing inequalities or pose significant risks if not managed consciously.

As scientists and engineers forge ahead in their quest to unearth the potential of Zero-Point Energy harvesting, fostering collaborative relationships across disciplines becomes a critical factor in addressing the multifaceted challenges at play. By creating alliances that include physicists, engineers, ethicists, and policymakers, we can ensure that the exploration of this quantum domain not only acknowledges the technology's potential but also remains firmly grounded in ethical considerations and societal well-being.

In summary, the prospects for energy harvesting from the Quantum Zero-Point Field hold immense potential to upend our current understanding of energy generation and consumption. By developing innovative approaches and materials aimed at extracting energy from the fringes of quantum mechanics, we may eventually unlock a sustainable energy source that could reshape our civilization's relationship with energy itself. However, it is essential to approach these developments with rigorous scientific inquiry, ethical consideration, and communal foresight, ensuring that the future of energy is not only powerful but also just and sustainable—an energy landscape that epitomizes the fullness of potential hidden within the emptiness of space.

5.2. Advancements in Quantum Computing

As we explore the uncharted territory of quantum computing, the connection to the Quantum Zero-Point Field unveils a landscape rich with potential. The inception of quantum computers—computational devices that leverage the principles of quantum mechanics—marks a revolutionary shift in computational capacity, moving us beyond the limitations of classical computers. At its core, quantum computing rests on the peculiar properties of qubits (quantum bits), which are capable of existing in multiple states simultaneously due to super-position. This extraordinary feature allows quantum computers to process vast quantities of information in parallel, surpassing conventional binary systems that restrict data processing to a single state at a time.

The Quantum Zero-Point Field plays a pivotal role in this quantum computational revolution. By existing as a field of energy even in an apparent vacuum, it imbues the quantum environment with fluctuations and interactions critical for the functioning of qubits. The interactions between qubits and the Zero-Point Field can enhance coherence times—an essential factor in ensuring the reliable performance of quantum computers. Coherence refers to the time during which qubits maintain their quantum state, and longer coherence times increase the fidelity of computations. Therefore, harnessing the Zero-Point Field and understanding its dynamics could lead to significant advancements in maintaining qubit stability, paving the way for robust and scalable quantum computers.

The dynamics of the Quantum Zero-Point Field also facilitate a greater understanding of error correction in quantum computing—one of the most significant challenges in the field. Quantum error correction is crucial for fault-tolerant quantum computing systems, as qubits are inherently susceptible to decoherence and external noise. By investigating how fluctuations from the Zero-Point Field interplay with qubit operations, researchers may uncover innovative strategies to mitigate errors and strengthen the resilience of quantum processing. This connection not only underscores the value of the Quantum Zero-Point Field as a resource but balances theoretical exploration with practical applications.

The implications extend beyond mere improvements in quantum computer performance. As researchers design algorithms exploiting the properties of quantum systems influenced by the Zero-Point Field, they could open the door to novel computing paradigms capable of solving problems currently deemed intractable. Fields such as cryptography, complex system simulations, and artificial intelligence could feel the transformative impact of such advancements. Quantum computers enabled by understanding the nuances of the Zero-Point Field could revolutionize our approach to data security, materials science, and algorithmic processes.

Moreover, the interface between quantum mechanics and the Zero-Point Field echoes potential pathways for achieving quantum supremacy—the point at which quantum computers perform tasks beyond the capabilities of the best classical supercomputers. The implications of reaching this milestone are profound, enticing fields from drug discovery to optimization problems, all of which could experience exponential boosts in processing capabilities driven by quantum technologies.

Beyond practical advancements, the intersection of quantum computing and the Quantum Zero-Point Field invites deeper philosophical reflections on the nature of computation, information, and reality itself. As quantum computing continues to evolve, it challenges our conventional understanding of information storage, retrieval, and processing—leading to a paradigm informed by principles of entanglement and non-locality. The Quantum Zero-Point Field serves as the bedrock upon which these principles flourish, reinforcing the idea that the universe is not merely a static entity but a dynamic web of interconnectivity and potential.

In conclusion, the advancements in quantum computing provide an exciting glimpse into the future of technology. The Quantum Zero-Point Field not only serves as a key factor in enhancing the performance and stability of quantum systems but also offers remarkable insights into the nature of computation and the underlying principles governing our universe. As we continue to unravel the complexities within quantum computing, we begin to see how harnessing the power of the Zero-Point Field can propel us into an era where the computational capabilities of humanity reach new heights, redefining our technological landscape and expanding the frontiers of knowledge and innovation.

5.3. Transformative Technologies

In the ever-evolving landscape of technology and innovation, understanding the Quantum Zero-Point Field has the potential to catalyze transformative advancements across multiple domains. This field, a sea of energy fluctuations that persist even in apparent voids, embodies possibilities that extend beyond mere theoretical musings. As researchers delve deeper into the nature of the Quantum Zero-Point Field, the implications for future technologies become increasingly tangible, suggesting new paths for energy generation, information processing, and material science, among others.

One of the most compelling prospects involves energy harvesting from the Zero-Point Field. Traditional energy systems rely heavily on finite resources, often contributing to detrimental impacts on the environment. However, the Zero-Point Field proposes an alternative narrative: energy exists ubiquitous and accessible, intrinsic to the fabric of space. Harnessing this energy could revolutionize our approach to power generation. Imagine technologies that could tap into the Zero-Point Field, converting quantum fluctuations into usable energy. Such innovations could lead to sustainable energy systems capable of powering cities, vehicles, and devices at minimal ecological cost, reshaping our relationship with energy consumption and availability.

The exploration of energy harvesting resonates deeply with ongoing advancements in materials science. As scientists develop metamaterials and smart materials designed to interact with the Quantum Zero-Point Field, the results may yield novel properties, from enhanced conductivity to previously unattainable strengths. These materials would serve as building blocks for next-generation applications —such as advanced electronics, telecommunications infrastructure, or even revolutionary construction materials capable of dynamic responsiveness to environmental factors. The cross-pollination between the understanding of quantum fields and advancements in material technology could pave the way for innovations that redefine industry standards.

Moreover, as we explore quantum computing—an area already intertwined with the Zero-Point Field—transformative technologies will likely emerge from manipulating qubits that draw upon quantum fluctuations. Future quantum computers may become not only exponentially faster than classical counterparts but would also possess the capability to solve complex problems across varied disciplines, from cryptography to climate modeling. These advancements could fundamentally alter how we handle data, utilize algorithms, and interface with artificially intelligent systems.

Interactions between the Quantum Zero-Point Field and quantum communication technologies also present exciting avenues for development. Secure communication channels that could rely on the principles of quantum entanglement promise an unprecedented level of cybersecurity. This could serve to protect sensitive information across various sectors, from finance to national defense, while enhancing global connectivity in ways previously limited to science fiction. Leveraging the Zero-Point Field may yield new protocols and systems that unlock secure, instantaneous data transfer across vast distances.

The integration of Zero-Point Energy concepts with artificial intelligence (AI) poses another potentially transformative dimension. The computational power of AI, coupled with the availability of boundless energy from the Zero-Point Field, could lead to the creation of advanced AI systems with greater cognitive capabilities. Such systems could redefine industries, revolutionizing healthcare, environmental management, and logistics, among others, thereby driving societal advancement in parallel with technological development.

As we navigate the complex interplay of these transformative technologies influenced by the understanding of the Quantum Zero-Point Field, it is critical to approach these developments with both optimism and caution. While the potential is staggering, each breakthrough must be carefully validated against rigorous scientific inquiry. A responsible approach ensures that speculative technologies do not bypass necessary testing and ethical considerations. Establishing frameworks for validation and assessment will enhance public trust and ensure these advancements serve the greater good.

In conclusion, understanding the Quantum Zero-Point Field is poised to unlock transformative technologies that could profoundly recast our relationship with energy, materials, and information systems. As we venture toward harnessing the latent potential within the quantum realm, we must embrace a mindset grounded in ethical considerations, scientific rigor, and collaborative innovation. The journey into the realms of the Quantum Zero-Point Field and the technologies it brings forth is not only a testament to human ingenuity but also an opportunity to redefine the trajectory of our world, inviting us to imagine the limitless possibilities that lie ahead.

5.4. Skepticism and Scientific Inquiry

The realm of skepticism and scientific inquiry serves as the cornerstone for advancing our understanding of complex concepts such as the Quantum Zero-Point Field and the possibilities it encompasses. As we traverse this intricate landscape, it is critical to acknowledge the role skepticism plays within the scientific method. Scientific inquiry thrives on testing hypotheses, gathering evidence, and refining theories based on empirical data, and skepticism ensures that claims are scrutinized and validated rather than accepted at face value. This process is essential, particularly when addressing concepts that challenge our fundamental understanding of energy, matter, and reality itself.

In the context of the Quantum Zero-Point Field, skepticism manifests in various forms. The very notion of extracting usable energy from this field, with its underpinnings deeply rooted in quantum mechanics, invites doubt. Some researchers argue that tapping into zero-point energy is unrealistic, given the constraints imposed by thermodynamics and conventional understandings of energy conservation. These skeptics contend that while it may be theoretically possible to conceive of such extraction, practical implementation remains elusive. This skepticism is not merely a hindrance; rather, it serves as a necessary counterbalance, compelling researchers to substantiate their claims with rigorous experimentation and validation before advancing the discourse further.

Historically, skepticism has propelled scientific inquiry across many fields. From the early days of quantum mechanics, where concepts such as wave-particle duality and uncertainty were met with disbelief, to contemporary debates surrounding the feasibility of quantum computing and the extraction of zero-point energy, a healthy degree of skepticism has acted as both a catalyst for rigorous research and a reminder of the intricacies involved in understanding the nature of the universe. Researchers must navigate uncertainties with caution, gathering empirical evidence to support their theories while remaining open to alternative interpretations and outcomes.

Scientific inquiry into the Quantum Zero-Point Field also necessitates interdisciplinary collaboration. Contributors from diverse domains— including physics, engineering, ethics, and philosophy—bring unique perspectives that can enrich the inquiry process. By fostering an environment where ideas can be debated, examined, and refined, the scientific community leads the exploration into the complexities of the zero-point field and its implications. This collaborative approach helps bridge gaps between theoretical concepts and tangible realities, facilitating progress toward practical applications and technological innovations.

Furthermore, the nature of quantum mechanics itself invites philosophical discussions that intertwine with scientific inquiry. The implications of the Zero-Point Field beckon us to reconsider our fundamental definitions of reality, energy, and existence. As researchers attempt to validate the energy present even in what was previously thought to be empty space, critical questions arise. What does it mean for our understanding of energy dynamics? How do these insights influence our perception of space as a mere void versus a vibrant field teeming with potential? Such discourse exemplifies the philosophical implications and challenges that scientific concepts often provoke.

The essential role of skepticism in scientific inquiry also raises important ethical considerations. As researchers delve into the potential applications of technology derived from the Quantum Zero-Point Field, ethical questions regarding energy exploitation, access, and sustainability inevitably emerge. The quest for new energy sources must be balanced with considerations of environmental impact, resource equity, and social responsibility. Skepticism, in this context, serves as a guiding principle for ethical scrutiny, ensuring that potential advancements prioritize the collective good rather than mere technological triumphs.

As we navigate the intersection of skepticism and scientific inquiry with the exploration of the Quantum Zero-Point Field, it is crucial to recognize that skepticism fosters a culture of inquiry capable of dismantling established paradigms while urging us toward deeper understandings. This balance represents the dynamism within the scientific method—an interplay that champions rigorous investigation, welcomes diverse perspectives, and embodies a commitment to enlightenment through inquiry.

Ultimately, the journey of exploring the Quantum Zero-Point Field, while ripe with promise, hinges upon our willingness to engage in critical examination and discourse. The marriage of skepticism and scientific inquiry serves to guide our explorations into the heart of energy dynamics, revealing a universe where profound energy exists within the seeming emptiness. With this guiding philosophy, we may one day harness that energy, all while redefining our understanding of existence and asserting our responsibility to navigate the complexities that lie ahead.

5.5. Ethics and Implications

The ethical considerations surrounding the exploration and potential applications of the Quantum Zero-Point Field and its associated technologies represent a multifaceted challenge, intertwining science, philosophy, social responsibility, and technology. As we venture deeper into the realm of quantum mechanics and energy harvesting, it is paramount to navigate the landscape with a keen awareness of the implications that arise from such pursuits. The transformation that quantum mechanics suggests—enabling the extraction of energy from what was once perceived as empty space—has far-reaching effects that warrant careful scrutiny.

First and foremost, the quest to harness Zero-Point Energy poses critical questions of sustainability. The allure of tapping into an unlimited and seemingly non-depleting energy source sparks excitement, proposing the possibility of a world where energy scarcity is eliminated. However, this promise demands diligent evaluation of how such energy could be utilized within our existing infrastructure. Transitioning to new energy paradigms necessitates an understanding of the environmental impacts associated with energy extraction, production methods, and potential consequences of exploitation. Irresponsible approaches to Zero-Point Energy could lead to unforeseen ecological disruptions, akin to the challenges we face in fossil fuel and mineral extraction practices. Thus, ensuring that energy harvesting aligns with sustainable practices is a prerequisite for ethical exploration.

Moreover, the socio-political implications of accessing such a potentially game-changing energy source cannot be ignored. The ability to leverage Zero-Point Energy could reshape global power dynamics, the economic landscape, and energy independence abroad. The question arises: who would control this energy? A handful of corporations, governments, or the broader population? Fostering equitable access to this new form of energy becomes essential to prevent further entrenchment of societal inequalities, particularly concerning energy resources. The ethical imperative lies in ensuring that advancements yield benefits for humanity as a whole rather than exacerbate existing disparities regarding access to energy and technology.

Additionally, the emergence of Quantum Zero-Point Energy technologies raises questions about ethical responsibilities embedded within scientific research. Scientists and technologists play a crucial role in guiding the trajectory of discovery and should be vigilant in their commitment to safeguarding societal interests. This responsibility extends to promoting transparency in research, fostering public understanding of the implications of these technologies, and incorporating diverse perspectives during development. Active engagement with stakeholders, including ethicists, policymakers, and community representatives, can help shape responsible practices that prioritize ethical stewardship of newfound energies.

Cognizance of the philosophical ramifications of Zero-Point Energy also plays a significant role in ethical discourse. The concept of emptiness is fundamentally challenged by the understanding that space, devoid of matter, can still harbor an abundance of energy. This philosophical transition redefines not only our understanding of energy dynamics but also our perception of existence itself. Engaging with such profound implications invites deeper inquiries into the nature of reality, consciousness, and interconnectedness—elements that underpin the ethical considerations of harnessing energy in a dynamically vibrant universe.

Ultimately, ethical considerations surrounding the Quantum Zero-Point Field and related technologies necessitate a proactive approach. Emphasizing interdisciplinary collaboration is essential; inviting discussions that engage scientists, ethicists, political leaders, and the community will cultivate rich dialogues that ensure ethical integrity throughout the exploration process. A responsible path forward involves recognizing the intricate tapestry of scientific opportunity and societal responsibility. Only by weaving these threads together can we illuminate the moral imperatives inherent in unlocking the potential of Zero-Point Energy while safeguarding the collective good.

As we transition from theoretical pursuit to practical application of technologies, we stand at a pivotal juncture—an opportunity to redefine our relationship with energy, existence, and ethical engagement in a landscape illuminated by the Quantum Zero-Point Field. This exploration beckons us to embrace a future grounded in responsibility, cooperation, and a commitment to ethical principles that honor the complex interplay between humanity and the cosmos. In a world where potentials meet responsibilities, we pave a path toward a sustainable and just future, harnessing the fullness of energy in the emptiness of space.

6. Philosophical Insights

6.1. Nature of Reality Re-examined

In an age where scientific inquiry and philosophical contemplation often intertwine, the examination of the Quantum Zero-Point Field provides a fertile ground for re-examining the nature of reality itself. This exploration inherently challenges the long-standing perceptions that have shaped human understanding for centuries, particularly in our conception of what constitutes existence, energy, and consciousness. The Zero-Point Field, representing an array of fluctuating energy present even in the absence of matter, invites us to rethink the implications of emptiness—a realm that classical physics treated as devoid of substance—into a dynamic and vibrant tapestry woven with possibility.

Traditionally, reality has been understood through a lens that respects physical phenomena as concrete and governable through established laws. Classical physics provides a framework that describes systems in deterministic terms, whereby the universe operates like a vast machine—a clock endowed with predictability and order. Here, emptiness was simply a vacuum, a backdrop to the real action observed in the movement of particles and forces in observable space. However, the advent of quantum mechanics and the introduction of quantized energy levels necessitated a shift in this understanding. The Quantum Zero-Point Field exposes the absurdity of considering 'nothingness' as trivial; rather, it teems with activity, housing complex interactions that bridge the gap between the physical and the abstract.

As we delve deeper into the implications of Zero-Point Energy, a major revelation surfaces: reality is not a static, neatly orchestrated arrangement of particles. Instead, it emerges as an intricate interweaving of probabilities, possibilities, and potentials that resonate through the very fabric of space. The continuous fluctuations inherent in the Zero-Point Field illustrate that what was once classified as empty is brimming with energy and dynamism. This shift brings into question not only the physics behind energy extraction—but also the philosophical ramifications tied to our perceptions of existence itself.

Moreover, grappling with these new understandings forces a re-evaluation of the observer's role in shaping reality. Quantum mechanics, particularly through principles like wave-particle duality and the uncertainty principle, suggests that the act of observation fundamentally alters the state of a system. This notion introduces profound philosophical inquiries about the interconnectedness of consciousness and reality. If consciousness can influence reality at the quantum level, what does this indicate about the relationship between observer and observed, subject and object? The implications ripple through metaphysical discussions, urging a re-examination of individual agency, ethics, and our responsibility to the cosmos, as we navigate the delicate balance between exploration and exploitation.

Moreover, the philosophical interpretations of the vacuum transcend scientific inquiry, inviting discussions on the nature of absence and presence itself. The Zero-Point Field invites existential ponderings, emphasizing that concepts of 'void' or 'nothingness' are replete with paradoxes—what appears to be empty is, in truth, an ocean of energy, hosting potential realities waiting to manifest. Thus, the realm of philosophical thought is challenged to posit new paradigms that reconcile experience, perception, and metaphysical inquiry with the emerging realities suggested by quantum physics.

In contemporary thought, this re-examination of the nature of reality and the exploration of quantum principles welcomes an array of interpretations. Thinkers across disciplines—scientists, philosophers, artists, and spiritual leaders—are drawn to the compelling dialogue between reality's intrinsic aspects and the implications derived from the Quantum Zero-Point Field. Notably, the appeal lies not only in the revolutionary scientific ideas but also in their capacity to inspire narratives that resonate with modern sensibilities—challenging our relationships with technology, existence, and even our interconnectedness as a global society.

Ultimately, the Quantum Zero-Point Field and its associated energy invite humanity to embrace a radical re-evaluation of existence, where the lines defining reality blur, giving way to new conceptual landscapes. As we traverse this terrain, we discover that the fullness of emptiness— teeming with energy, consciousness, and potential— affords an opportunity to cultivate a future enriched by ingenuity, respect, and an enlightened understanding of both science and philosophy. In recognizing the dynamism of existence within emptiness, we uncover profound truths about the interconnected nature of reality itself, promising transformative insights that could reshape humanity's journey through both consciousness and the cosmos. This journey beckons us to explore the depths of our inquiry, reminding us that in the broad expanse of the universe, nothing is truly empty, and every question leads us closer to the heart of everything.

6.2. Interconnection with Consciousness

The theoretical ties between consciousness and the Quantum Zero-Point Field provoke profound and intriguing questions about the nature of reality, awareness, and existence itself. As we venture into this intersection of quantum mechanics and philosophical inquiry, we find compelling parallels that challenge traditional assumptions about how we understand both mind and matter.

One of the most significant insights emerging from quantum mechanics suggests that observation plays a crucial role in the behavior of particles. In quantum physics, particles exist in a state of superposition—both being and not being—until they are measured. This act of observation influences the state of the particle, collapsing the wave function into a definite state. This phenomenon raises fascinating questions: Does consciousness itself act as an observer in this quantum realm, thereby participating in the formation of reality? The implications of such a notion bring to the forefront debates within both quantum physics and philosophy.

One prominent theory is that consciousness could be intricately linked to the fluctuations of the Quantum Zero-Point Field. If we consider consciousness as an emergent property of quantum interactions within our brain—specifically, as the mind arises from the collective behavior of quantum states—then arguably, the act of consciousness may have the potential to influence the quantum events around us. This idea aligns with interpretations proposed by figures such as physicist Eugene Wigner, who posited that consciousness could play a fundamental role in the measurement problem, thereby suggesting a deeper interconnection between mind and the quantum fabric of reality.

Furthermore, if consciousness shapes or influences quantum outcomes, this invites fresh inquiries into the relationship between individual perception and the broader universe. It compels us to consider whether our subjective realities are intricately woven into an objective existence, where our awareness not only reflects the environment but actively participates in its creation. This interconnection, then, challenges the dualistic separations often entrenched in philosophical thought, suggesting that the boundaries between observer and observed are inherently blurred.

Moreover, the implications extend from individual consciousness to collective consciousness—a concept suggesting that shared awareness or communal mental states might impact quantum phenomena at larger scales. Could the consciousness of many individuals synergize to influence outcomes in the Quantum Zero-Point Field? This perspective echoes ideas from transpersonal psychology and spiritual traditions that emphasize the interconnectedness of all beings, hinting at a universal consciousness transcending individual experiences, deeply rooted in the quantum realm.

In a broader philosophical context, these interconnections evoke inquiries into the nature of reality itself. If consciousness plays a role in shaping the fabric of existence, what underlying principles govern this interaction? The act of thinking—of perceiving, reflecting, and engaging with the world—may thus be seen as an integral part of the cosmos where thought and reality coalesce, raising questions about the validity and role of subjective experiences in understanding existence. This considerations prompt a reevaluation of existence as a co-created experience, where consciousness and matter are not distinct yet aligned forces but rather two sides of the same quantum coin.

Critically, navigating this landscape requires a careful approach. The synthesis of consciousness and the Quantum Zero-Point Field encourages experimentation in theoretical frameworks and empirical research while acknowledging their limitations; our understanding is far from definitive. As both consciousness and quantum mechanics remain elusive and inherently complex, speculation should foster inquiry rather than conclusion.

As we traverse this intellectual terrain, we find ourselves at the juncture of two tremendous domains—one that explores the quantum fabric of the universe and another that seeks to understand the nature of the human experience. The interconnection between consciousness and the Quantum Zero-Point Field beckons us to delve deeper into the mysteries that lie at the core of our existence. In exploring this synchronization, we uncover fresh perspectives on the mind's role in reshaping reality, hinting at an intricate relationship between awareness and the universe that calls for continued inquiry and contemplation.

Collectively, the study of interconnections between consciousness and the Quantum Zero-Point Field not only enriches scientific inquiry but also opens avenues for philosophical reflection, inviting us to reconsider the essence of reality, the purpose of consciousness, and the underlying unity between all aspects of existence.

6.3. Redefining 'Vacuum' in Philosophy

The study of quantum physics, particularly through the lens of the Quantum Zero-Point Field, leads to profound philosophical reinterpretations of what we consider to be 'vacuum.' Traditionally, 'vacuum' conveys the notion of emptiness, a void devoid of matter that accommodates our understanding of space and environment. However, as the intricacies of quantum mechanics unfold, the philosophical implications suggest that this interpretation is far from complete. The vacuum is not merely a barren expanse; rather, it emerges as a dynamic field brimming with energy and potentialities that redefine our consciousness and understanding of reality.

In classical philosophy, the vacuum has often been characterized by absence. Thinkers like Aristotle championed the idea that nature detests a vacuum, rejecting the notion that empty space could exist independently. For Aristotle and many of his contemporaries, what exists must embody some essence or form, and thus, the idea of emptiness as a stand-alone reality clashed with prevailing thoughts about the nature of being. In this light, 'vacuum' was synonymous with a lack of substance—a conceptual dead end that bore little relevance to the fabric of existence.

Conversely, as the Quantum Zero-Point Field emerges as a defining element within modern physics, we are compelled to re-examine these philosophical notions. The vacuum, as understood in classical terms, begins to blur with the realities presented by quantum mechanics. Instead of denoting nothingness, the vacuum of space is alive with fluctuating energies. Virtual particles flicker in and out of existence, rising from and disappearing into the Quantum Zero-Point Field, illustrating that emptiness is replete with activity. This engaging profile of the vacuum marks a radical departure from earlier interpretations, insisting instead that the nature of reality is fundamentally dynamic and interconnected.

The implications of this redefinition extend into diverse realms of thought, encompassing not only physics but also theology, art, and cognitive science. Each discipline wrestles with the entwinement of existence and non-existence, prompting reflections on the nature of being itself. Philosophers such as Whitehead embraced the concept of process philosophy, wherein reality is understood more as a series of events and processes, prompting profound inquiry into how we might define existence and essence in a universe characterized by perpetual change.

Moreover, as we seek to understand the nuances of the quantum vacuum, a key philosophical challenge beckons the question of how observer dynamics interplay with the state of the universe. If consciousness can influence particles and their behaviors, what does that portend for our understanding of existence itself? The interplay between conscious observation and the physical world suggests a co-creative partnership between mind and the cosmos; reality becomes a dynamic manifestation shaped by myriad interactions rather than a static tableau. This invites us to contemplate our role within the universe, connecting the dots between philosophical inquiry and empirical discovery.

Additionally, contemporary thinkers are galvanized by the implications of redefining vacuum in philosophy. The concept encourages dialogues across disciplines—merging insights from quantum physics with metaphysics, ethics, and existentialism. Figures in modern philosophy like Martin Heidegger have traversed these exploratory paths, venturing into the heart of being and non-being, offering resonances with quantum understandings of the vacuum and existence. The insights gained from the Quantum Zero-Point Field resonate with discourses on consciousness, urging renewed perspectives on what it means to exist in a universe fraught with potentials.

As societies advance into this new realm of thought, philosophical explorations pertaining to 'empty spaces' challenge foundational beliefs historically rooted in classical frameworks. Contemporary dialogues reveal a rich tapestry composing the cosmos, urging us to re-conceive our place in the grand scheme of things. This philosophical discourse emphasizes that the void is not merely a lack, but rather a crucible for creativity and potential—honoring the fullness within emptiness.

In summary, redefining 'vacuum' from a philosophical standpoint invites us to reconsider entrenched ideas about existence and non-existence. The Quantum Zero-Point Field illuminates a reality where emptiness is a dynamic entity, rich in energy, fluctuation, and potential. This shift has profound implications resonating through modern thought, urging interdisciplinary connections and philosophical inquiries that redefine our understanding of the universe, consciousness, and our integral role within its majestic tapestry. As we continue to explore these notions, we uncover the fullness of the cosmos lying within what appears to be empty space, transforming our narrative into one that celebrates interconnectedness, potential, and the vibrancy of existence itself.

6.4. Influence on Modern Thought

The impact of the Quantum Zero-Point Field on modern thought is both profound and multi-faceted, creating ripples across various intellectual domains. As scientists and philosophers alike wrestle with the implications of this field, a shift in paradigms is taking place that influences not only technical disciplines but also the broader existential inquiries about existence, consciousness, and the nature of reality itself.

The Quantum Zero-Point Field suggests that space is not merely an empty vacuum but a rich arena pulsating with energy and potential. This realization challenges long-held views rooted in classical physics and traditional philosophy. In classical thinking, the vacuum was viewed as a lifeless void, simply the absence of matter. However, as quantum mechanics reveals that even "empty" space is teeming with fluctuations, the understanding of emptiness evolves into one that carries with it a sense of abundance and activity.

Within scientific domains, this shift has encouraged deeper inquiry into the nature of reality. Physicists are exploring the ways in which quantum fluctuations contribute to physical phenomena, reshaping our understanding of interactions, forces, and energy. Research into harnessing Zero-Point Energy represents a cutting-edge trajectory that could lead to new technologies, sustainability efforts, and energy paradigms. Scientists are now venturing beyond traditional boundaries and investigating ideas that were once relegated to speculation, thus encouraging a culture of creativity and innovation within the scientific community.

Moreover, the implications extend to philosophical inquiry, compelling scholars to engage with the fundamental questions surrounding existence and consciousness. Philosophers are increasingly drawn to the notion that consciousness may play a crucial role in shaping reality at the quantum level. Discussions surrounding the observer effect challenge established dichotomies between subject and object, raising inquiries about the highly interconnected nature of existence. The idea that consciousness might influence the quantum domain elevates discourse surrounding not just philosophical implications but ethical considerations about our relationship with the cosmos.

As thinkers reflect on these interconnected ideas, contemporary philosophy is witnessing a renaissance that embraces holistic approaches. Rather than adhering to reductionist perspectives, modern theorists are weaving together narratives that incorporate science, spirituality, and psychology. This synthesis exemplifies an expansive view of knowledge that values diverse methodologies, enhancing our understanding of reality as an intricate web of interactions.

Additionally, the intersection of the Quantum Zero-Point Field with other domains—such as neuroscience, cognitive science, and artificial intelligence—gives rise to interdisciplinary explorations that seek to elucidate the complexities of human consciousness. Insights from quantum mechanics are intertwining with explorations into how we perceive reality, how thoughts manifest into actions, and the energetic connections among individuals and the broader universe.

In artistic realms, the philosophical insights drawn from the Quantum Zero-Point Field inspire a new wave of creative expression. Artists are reflecting on notions of potentiality, transformation, and interconnectedness, offering reflections on the human experience as a dynamic and ever-evolving narrative. As they contemplate the fullness of what seems to be void, they challenge viewers to reconsider their own perceptions of existence and recognize the beauty in both emptiness and abundance.

Moreover, the influence of the Quantum Zero-Point Field extends to collective human consciousness, prompting urgent discussions surrounding responsibility and ethical stewardship. In a world increasingly aware of ecological concerns and social inequalities, the philosophical underpinnings derived from the Zero-Point Field encourage a re-assessment of our approaches to innovation and energy consumption. As we explore the potentials within quantum fields, it is our ethical obligation to ensure that such advancements serve humanity's collective well-being rather than exacerbate existing disparities.

From a broader societal perspective, the influence of these ideas fuels a vision of unity and respect for the interconnectedness of all beings. As contemporary thought grapples with the implications of the Quantum Zero-Point Field, it underscores a narrative of potentiality that embraces compassion, cooperation, and shared responsibilities. The recognition that consciousness plays a fundamental role in shaping reality cultivates a deeper understanding of our interconnected destinies, inviting thoughtful considerations about how we coexist within the intricate tapestry of existence.

Ultimately, the influence of the Quantum Zero-Point Field on modern thought resonates in a multitude of ways, evoking deep inquiries into the nature of reality and our place within it. As scientists explore, philosophers reflect, artists create, and societies adapt to these transformative insights, we approach the possibility of reshaping our understanding of existence itself. The journey through the complexities and potentials of the Zero-Point Field illuminates not only the scientific endeavor but inherently challenges us all to explore the fullness of life within the vast expanses of apparent emptiness. In beckoning us to venture deeper into the mysteries of the universe, the Quantum Zero-Point Field instills a sense of wonder that propels humanity forward on its quest for knowledge, understanding, and connection.

6.5. Exploration of 'Empty Spaces'

Empty spaces, traditionally perceived as voids devoid of substance, take on new dimensions within the context of the Quantum Zero-Point Field. This contemplation invites us to rethink everything we associate with emptiness, linking it intricately to the quantum mechanics that govern our universe. This exploration merges the scientific inquiry into the nature of energy and matter with profound philosophical implications, leading to a richer understanding of reality itself.

As we delve into these 'empty spaces,' we encounter the Quantum Zero-Point Field—a reservoir of energy existing even in the absence of matter. In classical physics, emptiness implies a lack, an absence of light, sound, energy, or any observable phenomenon. However, the understanding of quantum mechanics shatters this dichotomy. The so-called vacuum is not an inactive backdrop but a dynamic realm filled with potential. Quantum fluctuations occur within this field, constantly affecting the behavior of particles and revealing that empty space is alive with energy.

When we consider these empty spaces from a philosophical standpoint, we realize they challenge our conventional understanding of existence. If a vacuum brims with energy and spontaneous particle creation, then what does this imply for our perceptions of life, consciousness, and the cosmos? Philosophers have historically grappled with questions about the nature of existence: Is something that cannot be perceived or measured still part of reality? The insights emerging from quantum physics suggest an affirmative answer. The mere act of observing or measuring creates a manifestation of reality, thus illustrating the interconnectedness of consciousness and existence.

The idea that consciousness itself can influence quantum states compels us to consider our role in shaping reality. If these empty spaces are not as void but filled with possibilities, this revelation invokes an ethical responsibility for how we engage with the world. It prompts questions about the intentionality of thought, the power of observation, and the interconnected web of existence in which we participate. Under this view, every thought or intention radiates within the fabric of the quantum field, potentially influencing the outcome of events, thereby shedding light on the notion of mindfulness and the necessity of ethical living.

Furthermore, revisiting empty spaces through the lens of the Quantum Zero-Point Field reflects a needed paradigm shift—a movement away from reductionistic approaches that see the universe primarily in mechanical terms, towards holistic perspectives that embrace complexity, interconnectedness, and the intrinsic vibrancy of the universe. Contemplating empty spaces as sites of potential elevates our understanding of energy flows, possibility, and the creative aspects of the cosmos itself.

In art and literature, these themes resonate with an invitation for expression that embraces the interplay of absence and presence. Artists often delve into the emotional and existential implications of emptiness, inviting viewers to explore their interpretations of voids and spaces in their life. The Quantum Zero-Point Field adds a layer of complexity to this dialogue, suggesting that what may physically appear empty can reverberate with emotional depth and significance. Artists may draw inspiration from this quantum understanding, capturing the vibrancy and dynamism inherent in the spaces around them.

Engaging with empty spaces leads us to confront our own perceptions of the world and the extent of our comprehension of reality. It catalyzes inquiry into not only the scientific implications of energy and matter but also the philosophical, ethical, and artistic interpretations that surround our relationship with the cosmos. In embracing the fullness found within the emptiness, we open ourselves to a profound understanding that fosters empathy and interconnectedness among all beings.

As we continue to navigate the philosophical discourse on empty spaces in relation to the Quantum Zero-Point Field, it becomes clear that our interpretations will forever shape the narrative of existence itself. These explorations urge us to appreciate the subtleties of life, the vibrancy within what appears void, and the infinite possibilities that lie within our reach. Understanding empty spaces as dynamic realms enhances not only scientific inquiry but also enriches our experience as conscious participants in a universe resonating with potential and fullness, awaiting our perceptions and engagement. This journey compels us not only to ponder the depths of emptiness but also to embrace its implications for our understanding of reality, consciousness, and our place within this wondrous universe.